Felt *with love*

FELT HEARTS, FLOWERS AND MUCH MORE

Madeleine Millington

First published in Great Britain 2013

Search Press Limited
Wellwood, North Farm Road,
Tunbridge Wells, Kent TN2 3DR

Reprinted 2013

ISBN: 978-1-84448-769-1

Suppliers
For details of suppliers, please visit the Search Press website: www.searchpress.com.

You are invited to visit the author's website: www.madeleinemillington.com

Publisher's note:
All the step-by-step photographs in this book feature the author, Madeleine Millington. No models have been used.

Dedication
Andrew, Anna, Sophie and Tom

Acknowledgements
I would like to thank Roz Dace for encouraging me to do this book; Alison Shaw and Katie French for guiding me through; and Paul Bricknell for his expert photography and good humour. Also my family, who have always encouraged me and have been surrounded by dyed blankets for most of their lives! Last but not least, Sonja Head and Pat Sales for their expert tutoring and encouragement all those years ago and who opened my eyes to the riches of embroidery and design.

Contents

Projects

Introduction

I have been working with gorgeous fabrics now for over twenty years. My first project was a large-scale wall piece, but I couldn't find exactly the right colours that I needed. This was when I embarked on learning how to dye old wool blankets in the washing machine – and the rest, as they say, is history.

Inspiration comes from looking – patterns and colours are everywhere. Folk Art, with its enormous richness, is a great source of inspiration for me, and it is the simplicity of this style coupled with the use of old or recycled fabrics that produces such exciting, rustic results. Folk Art is inventive and uses readily available materials, which makes for a very satisfying and inexpensive craft adventure.

The projects in this book can be made from all sorts of felt: synthetic felt, wool felt or felted fabrics such as a wool blanket, an old tweed skirt or a scarf. Everything can be made by simply following the step-by-step instructions and pictures provided, and you don't need to have any previous experience. The projects are here to inspire you, so make them exactly as they appear on the page or adapt them to suit your own taste. For example, the Tree Top Bird (page 68) could look equally charming on the front of a cushion cover.

Appliqué is the name given to the decorative technique of sewing fabric shapes on to another piece of material, and it has been around in some form for as long as humans have been able to use a needle and thread. Felt is particularly good for appliqué, as the build up of layers and different textures can produce exciting results. I love working with wool felt in particular because it is so soft and pliable. Wool felt has a wonderful surface to stitch on; the stitches sink into the fabric to give it an almost quilted look. Another great feature of felt is that you do not have to turn the edges under, which makes for less work and means that the projects grow quickly. There is certainly something very pleasing about working with this charming fabric.

The step-by-step projects in this book will enable you to create colourful and highly original decorative items that you can keep for yourself or give away to someone special. In this hectic world of mass-produced products there is nothing quite like presenting someone with a hand-crafted gift, or making something festive to match your Christmas decorations. I hope you will have as much fun stitching the projects in this book as I have had designing and making them up. Create, decorate and celebrate.

Happy stitching!

Materials & equipment

The materials and equipment needed for the projects in this book are very simple indeed, and in this section I have outlined the basic requirements. All the stitching is done by hand, which means that you can work on projects when away from home, travelling or just sitting in a cosy corner. I have used a sewing machine to stitch the cushion together (see page 50), but even this could be hand stitched if you don't have a machine available.

A selection of dyed wool felt and tweeds.

Felt fabric

There are many shop-bought felt fabrics readily available. These range from synthetic, mixed-fibre felts through to wool felt. Synthetic and mixed-fibre varieties are cheaper and thinner than wool felt. Though wool felt is wonderfully soft and gorgeous to work with, it is more expensive. It can be fun to mix up the different qualities of fabrics to give richer textures.

I also enjoy using wool fabrics that I have felted myself because they have such a wonderful tactile surface, particularly when stitched or appliquéed. The layers, stitches and embellishments sink right into them, producing a lovely quilted quality. There is a wide variety of wool fabrics on the market these days, and I particularly love using old wool blankets, which I dye. You could also recycle the fabric from old wool skirts and jackets. Experiment!

Needles

Use a darning or sharp chenille needle when working with the double knitting-wool yarn, making sure the needle has a large enough eye to take the thickness of the thread. For the projects using cotton perlé or stranded cotton thread you can use any needle, so long as it is sharp and accommodates the thickness of the thread, allowing it to pass through the eye of the needle easily. A beading needle is used for some projects where a single strand of stranded cotton is being used.

Threads

A variety of threads has been used throughout the book. Where the project has required a bold, chunky look I have used double knitting-wool yarn. Where the project requires a finer thread, then I have mostly used cotton perlé or a stranded cotton (two strands) in a variety of colours. It is a good idea to use high-quality thread as it is stronger and will last longer.

Colourful selection of threads used in the projects throughout the book.

Embellishments

Embellishments can be great fun to use, and most of us have plenty of them stashed away. Suggestions and examples have been used in the projects, but feel free to add an extra button or omit the sequins to suit your personal taste. Buttons, beads, sequins, ribbon, wire and cords can all be used to great effect, and you could even take them from old bags or pieces of clothing.

Other materials

A small selection of extra materials has also been used to complete the projects. Most things, like pins, string, strong glue, a ruler and curtain rings, can be easily found around the house. In some cases I have tried to be as economical as possible by using things like card from a cereal box where stiffening is required, and an old colouring pencil to apply the rosy cheeks on the Garland of Angels project (page 72). It is also wise to invest in good-quality scissors so that the larger pieces of fabric can be cut neatly and accurately, as well as a sharp, smaller pair for the more intricate cutting. If you wish to dye your own fabrics then protective gloves, fabric dye and salt will also be needed.

Collecting together and preparing your materials carefully before you start a project ensures a good end result.

Dyeing fabrics

I have always dyed my own fabrics as I enjoy the freedom I get from being in control of my colour palette. It can also lead to surprises along the way, especially when dyeing fabrics of different thicknesses or fibre mixes.

I prefer to dye fabrics using the washing machine. This method gives an excellent, even, all-over colour – especially for large pieces of fabric. For the projects in this book, however, small-scale hand dyeing is perfectly adequate and simple. You can obtain a good range of gorgeous colours and there are several good-quality wool dyes on the market. Having purchased a suitable dye, follow the manufacturer's instructions, making sure that the fabric is thoroughly wet before it is immersed in the dye.

The equipment you will need is minimal: a pair of protective gloves, a plastic container in which to dye the fabric, a measuring jug, a spoon to stir with and, in most cases, some salt. Rinse the fabric very well after dyeing, as this helps to remove all the loose dye.

Over-dyeing

There are opportunities to experiment and have some fun with fabric dyeing, and over-dyeing is one of them. Take various samples of patterned and coloured wool fabric such as tweed, checked, striped or plain and put them into a dye bath. In this case (below) I have used a turquoise dye. The result is an exciting collection which can be interspersed with other plain colours, or could work well together using a restrained colour scheme.

Changing the shade and depth of colour

Another way of experimenting with dye is to vary the ratio of dye to fabric. Various shades and depths of colour can be achieved, giving you a more adventurous palette to work with.

Fabrics dyed with varying strengths of different coloured dyes.

Different fabrics dyed with turquoise dye.

The hand-dyeing process

Use these hand-dyeing instructions as a guide only; refer to the manufacturer's guidelines on the packet of dye for more detailed instructions.

You will need, a plastic or pyrex container that will hold 6 litres (12½ pints), protective gloves, fabric for dyeing, a measuring jug, powder fabric dye, water, salt and a spoon.

The dyed fabric

1 Take your fabric and wet it in lukewarm water. Wring out the excess water and leave damp for dyeing.

2 Using protective gloves to protect your hands, dissolve approximately 50g (1¾oz) of powder dye in the colour of your choice in a measuring jug of about 500ml (17½ fl oz) of warm water.

3 Fill a container with approximately 6 litres (12½ pints) of warm water and stir in 250g (8¾oz) of salt. Allow the salt to dissolve in the water.

4 Add the jug of dye to the water and stir well.

5 Submerge the fabric in the dye, stir for about 15 minutes and then stir regularly for approximately 45 minutes to agitate the fabric and allow the dye to penetrate the fabric evenly.

6 After an hour, remove the fabric from the container of dye and rinse it well in cold water. Wash the fabric in warm water and a little detergent and leave to dry.

Stitches

Throughout this book I have used some simple stitches. Some are practical, like overstitch, which is used for sewing pieces of fabric together, and others are used for decoration, for example star stitch and running stitch. I prefer to use decorative stitching in a simple way, often using a contrasting coloured thread to bring extra attention to the detail.

Overstitch

1   Bring the needle up next to the edge of the fabric you want to stitch in place.

2   Insert the needle down into the fabric you are attaching and pull the thread through.

3   The finished overstitch. Repeat around all of the edges to secure.

Running stitch

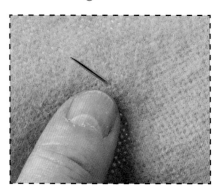  

1   Bring the needle up through the back of the fabric where you want to start stitching.

2   Insert the needle down into the fabric a short distance away and bring it back up again, leaving a similar gap.

3   The finished running stitch. Repeat to achieve the desired effect, making the stitches as long or short as you like.

Cross stitch

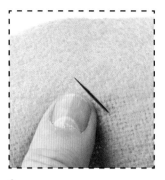   

1   Bring the needle up at the top left point of the cross.

2   Take the needle back down at the bottom right point of the cross.

3   Take the thread across the back and come up at the bottom left point. Go across the front and down at the top right point.

4   The finished cross stitch.

Star stitch

  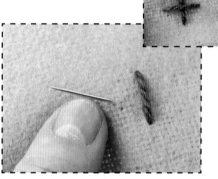

1   Bring the needle up at the top point of the star.

2   Take the needle down at the bottom point.

3   Take the thread across the back and come up at the left point. Go across the front and down at the right point.

4   Take the thread across the back and come up at the top left corner. Go across the front and down at the bottom right corner.

5   Take the thread across the back and come up at the bottom left corner, go across the front and down at the top right.

6   The finished star stitch.

Couching

   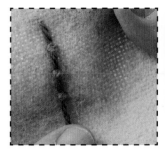

1 Bring the needle up through the fabric where you want the design to begin.

2 Lay down the thread and bring a separate thread up on one side.

3 Take the needle down on the other side of the laid-down thread.

4 Make a stitch over the laid-down thread and come up on the first side to start the second stitch. Continue making stitches until your design is complete.

Fly stitch

 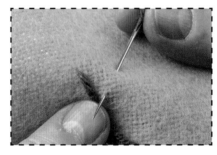 

1 Bring the needle through the back of the fabric at the top left corner of the 'Y'-shaped stitch.

2 Hold the thread down at the base of the 'V' and insert the needle a small distance away to the right of where the thread came through. Bring the needle back through at the base of the 'V'.

3 With the thread passing under the needle, pull the thread through.

4 Insert the needle back down directly below to make the tying stitch and create a 'Y' shape.

5 The finished fly stitch.

French knot

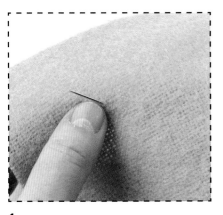

1 Bring the needle to the surface in the stitch position.

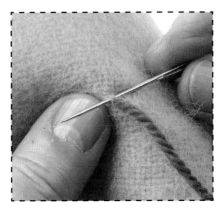

2 Pick up a tiny piece of the background fabric with the needle. Do not pull the needle through.

3 Wrap the thread around the needle three or four times.

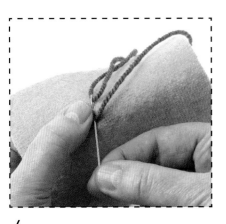

4 Hold the wrappings in place securely with your left thumb and pull the thread through.

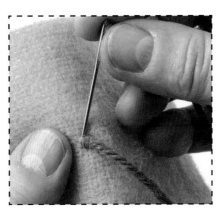

5 Take the needle down through the fabric to secure the knot.

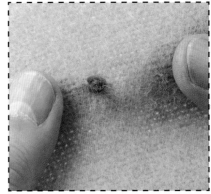

6 The finished French knot.

French knots are used to give texture to the hair on the angel (see page 73).

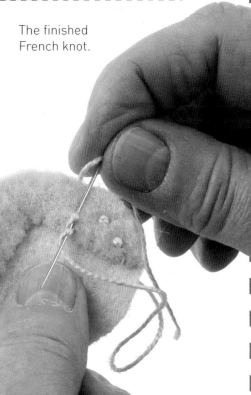

Blanket stitch

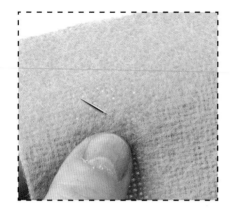

1 Bring the needle up through the fabric where you want the line of stitches to begin.

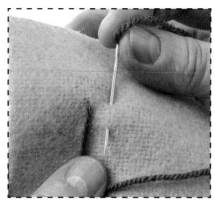

2 Hold the thread down with your left thumb and insert the needle a small distance to the right, level with where the thread came through. Make a downwards stitch under the fabric.

3 Take the needle over the thread and pull the thread through.

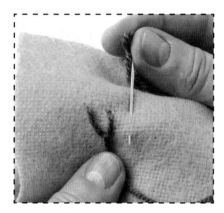

4 Hold the thread down with your left thumb and make another downwards stitch, as before.

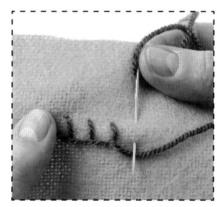

5 Repeat the stitch for as long as necessary. Blanket stitch is usually employed on the edges of fabric.

Use blanket stitch to sew the two sides of a felt shape together before stuffing.

Stem stitch

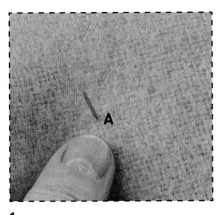

1 Bring the needle to the front of the fabric where you want the line of stitches to begin (point A).

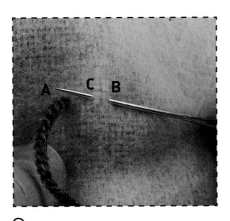

2 With the thread below the line of stitching, insert the needle a short distance to the right at point B, and bring it through halfway back towards A at point C.

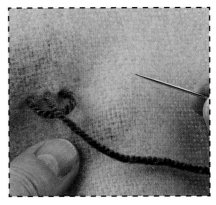

3 Pull the thread through.

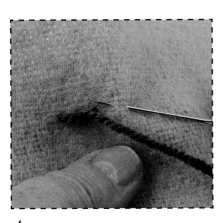

4 Make another stitch to the right, keeping the sewing thread under the stitch line as before.

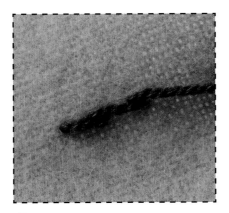

5 Continue stitching for as long as necessary.

Stem stitch is used to embroider the features on the face of the princess (see page 80).

Adding embellishments

Beads

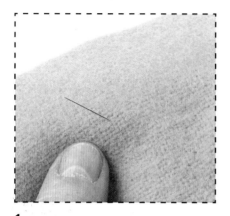

1 Insert a beading needle from the back of the fabric through to the front and pull the thread through.

2 Pick up a bead with the point of the needle and take the needle down to the back close to where it came through.

3 Repeat this process to stitch on as many beads as desired.

Curtain rings

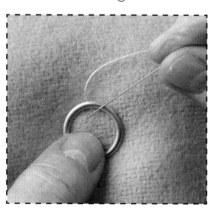

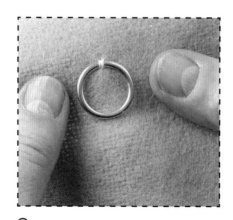

1 Bring the needle up through the fabric on the outer edge of the curtain ring and take it back down next to the inner edge.

2 Repeat this stitch several times until the ring is secured safely.

Sequins

1 Insert a threaded needle from the back of the fabric through to the front.

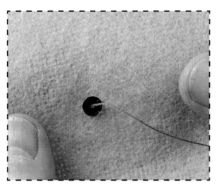

2 Pick up a sequin with the point of the needle and push it down to the end of the thread.

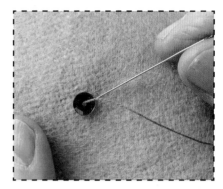

3 Insert the needle back down into the fabric close to the edge of the sequin.

4 Bring the needle back up again on the other side of the sequin.

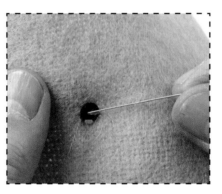

5 Take the needle down into the fabric through the centre of the sequin.

6 Repeat this process to stitch on as many sequins as desired.

Buttons

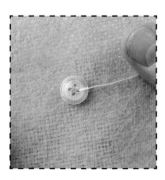

1 Insert a needle from the back of the fabric and thread on a button.

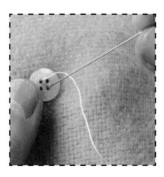

2 Insert the needle back down into the fabric through the diagonally opposite hole in the button.

3 Bring the needle back up again through one of the remaining holes.

4 Push the needle back down through the final hole to secure the button in place.

Hanging Flower

This is a simple, fun project which could be done in many different colour schemes and used to decorate your home all year round. Here I have used fresh spring colours, but white, red and green would make a pretty Christmas tree decoration. Look at the flowers in your garden or the florist's shop for different colour combinations to develop your ideas further. You might be surprised at Mother Nature's colour palette!

YOU WILL NEED

Templates: Flower 1, Flower 2, Circle 1 and Circle 2

Felt in yellow, blue, orange and pale green

Thread: cotton perlé thread in yellow, orange, green, purple and variegated orange; and white machine thread

Needles: sharp chenille and beading

Pins

Fabric scissors

Glass seed beads in pink

Purple cord

Thin card

1 Cut out the felt shapes using the templates: two of Flower 1 – one in blue and one in green; Flower 2 in yellow; Circle 2 in orange and Circle 1 in pale green. Lay the yellow flower on top of the blue flower and pin in place.

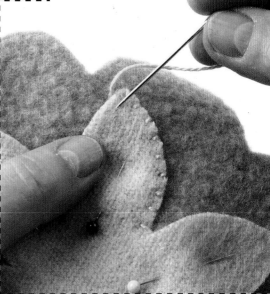

2 Using cotton perlé thread in yellow and a sharp chenille needle, overstitch all around the yellow petals to secure the yellow flower in place.

3 Pin the orange circle to the centre of the yellow flower. Overstitch all around the edge using orange cotton perlé thread to secure it in place.

4 Pin the green circle to the centre of the small orange circle. Overstitch all around the edge to secure, using green cotton perlé thread.

5 Using a beading needle and white machine thread, stitch a sprinkling of pink glass seed beads to the green circle, following the technique on page 18.

6 Return to the sharp chenille needle and, using a variegated orange cotton perlé thread, work running stitch up the centre of each yellow petal. This embellishment gives the impression of veins running through each petal.

7 Take a length of purple cord approximately 27cm (10¾in) long and fold in half. Tie a knot at one end to make the cord into a loop from which to hang the flower.

8 Attach the cord to the back of the stitched blue flower using purple cotton perlé thread and a few overstitches.

9   Using the blue flower as a guide, cut out a piece of thin card in the same shape, but slightly smaller than the flower.

10   Sandwich the card flower between the back of the stitched blue flower and the green flower backing.

11   Pin all the layers together to secure.

12   Starting near to the purple cord and, using cotton perlé thread in purple, blanket stitch all the way around the flower to join the front and back together. Use evenly spaced stitches and make sure you are working through both felt layers. The stitches used here are joining or construction stitches rather than decorative ones, but still aim to keep them as tidy as possible.

Floating Floral Fun

Hang these flowers in your car, on doorknobs, in the window... anywhere that needs a bit of colour! Experiment with the length of the cord to create a dynamic display.

Flower Trio

This trio of bright and bold flowers will brighten up any room. Place them all together in a vase or other container, or individually in a row for a more contemporary look. I have introduced checks and tweeds for a more exciting, varied colour scheme, but plain coloured felts work just as well.

YOU WILL NEED

- Templates: Flower 1, Flower 3, Circle 3, Circle 4 and Circle 5
- Felt in turquoise, red, blue and lilac
- Thread: cotton perlé thread in red, lilac and turquoise; satin thread in lime green; and variegated cotton perlé thread in orange/yellow
- Needles: sharp chenille
- Pins
- Fabric scissors
- Thin card
- Old wooden knitting needle, thin bamboo garden cane or similar
- Matt emulsion paint in pale green
- Strong glue

1 Cut out two of Flower 1 in turquoise (one for the front and one for the back); Flower 3 in lilac; Circle 3 in red; Circle 4 in turquoise; and eight of Circle 5 in blue. Lay the red felt circle, centred, on top of one of the turquoise flowers and pin it in place.

2 Overstitch the red circle to the centre of the turquoise flower using red cotton perlé thread and a sharp chenille needle. Make each stitch individually, parallel to each other, as this will give you a neater edge. Stitch all the way around the red circle to secure.

3 Lay the small lilac flower in the centre of the red circle and pin it in place. Overstitch around the small flower to secure it using lilac cotton perlé thread.

4 Lay the eight tiny blue circles at the tip of each of the petals on the small lilac flower. Position them so that they slightly overlap the edges of the petals.

5 Attach the tiny circles one at a time using the lilac cotton perlé thread. Overstitch all the way around each tiny circle.

6 Take the small turquoise felt circle and pin it in place in the centre of the lilac flower. Overstitch in place all the way around the edge using lime green satin thread.

7 Take a length of variegated orange/yellow thread across the petal from the edge of the turquoise circle to one of the tiny blue circles. Make a straight stitch. Use the turquoise cotton perlé thread to couch down the variegated thread (see page 14).

8 Repeat until you have couched lines on each petal. Using the lime green satin thread, stitch a decorative line of running stitch around the centre circle.

9 Paint your wooden knitting needle/thin bamboo cane with pale green paint and leave to dry. Cut out a piece of thin card using the template Flower 1, but slightly smaller. Using strong glue, attach the stick to the card flower and allow to dry.

10 Sandwich the card and stick between the stitched turquoise flower and the unstitched turquoise flower, and pin the two felt pieces together. Blanket stitch all around the edge of the flowers in turquoise cotton perlé thread. When you reach the stick, blanket stitch across the top flower only and leave the bottom layer unstitched. Continue stitching around the remainder of the flower.

Flower Garland

Garlands and flowers play an important part in Folk Art. They can be found decorating walls, furniture and textiles. This very pretty decoration can be made to be used all year round or for a particular celebration. Try pink, white and green flowers for a wedding, the colours of a national flag for a patriotic theme, or green and red for Christmas. With a hint of spring or a promise of warm summer days, bring the outdoors indoors with this lovely decoration.

YOU WILL NEED

Templates: Flower 3, Circle 1, Circle 2 and Leaf 1

Felt in assorted colours of your choice and pale green for the leaves

Buttons in assorted colours of your choice

Thread: cotton perlé thread in colours to match the felt

Needles: sharp chenille

Pins

Fabric scissors

Curtain rings

1 Using the templates, cut out a felt flower and two different-sized felt circles in colours of your choice. Lay the smaller circle inside the larger one and place them on top of the flower. Position a button in the centre of the smallest circle. Using matching cotton perlé thread, stitch the button in place to secure all the layers together.

2 Using assorted colours of felt, make as many flowers as you wish to make up a flower garland to the length you desire. For each alternating flower, use the leaf template to cut out a leaf shape from pale green felt and position it under the flower shape, stitching it in place with all the other layers when you attach the button.

3   To attach each flower to another, stitch a few overstitches between two petals to join them securely.

4   The join should look like this from the front.

5   Attach a curtain ring to the back of the last flower at each end of your garland so that you can hang it easily. Follow the instructions on page 18 to do this.

Fanciful Flowers

This garland of flowers would look perfect draped across a bookshelf or doorway, or hung above the bed.

Brooches

What to do with all the scraps? These lovely brooches are an ideal way to use up all the bits left over from the projects. They can be worn on clothing or pinned to a bag for a personal touch.

The instructions below refer to the heart brooch; the flower and bird are made in exactly the same way. The templates for these are provided on page 88.

YOU WILL NEED

Templates: Heart 1 and
    Circle 5
Felt in orange, purple, yellow
    and aquamarine
Thread: cotton perlé thread
    in lime green and lilac;
    and silk thread in
    bright pink
Needles: sharp chenille
Pins
Fabric scissors
Pinking shears
Thin card
Small pearl button
Brooch fastening

1

Cut out a 5cm (2in) square of orange felt, and use the templates to cut out a small purple heart and a tiny yellow circle. Pin the heart to the centre of the orange square and overstitch all the way around the outside edge using cotton perlé thread in lime green and a sharp chenille needle.

2   Attach the tiny yellow felt circle to the centre of the purple heart and, using the same lime green thread and needle, overstitch it in place all the way around the edge of the circle.

3   Using bright pink silk thread, work running stitch on to the heart around the outside of the circle for decoration.

4   Using cotton perlé thread in lilac, attach the button to the centre of the yellow circle as an embellishment.

5   Carefully cut out the heart from the orange felt, leaving a narrow orange border.

6   Use the heart template to cut out a smaller heart from thin card. Place the card heart on the back of the stitched heart.

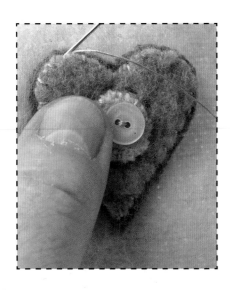

7 Lay the heart on the aquamarine felt, with the card heart sandwiched in between, and stitch the two layers together using a small running stitch around the edge of the purple heart. Use lilac cotton perlé thread. Make sure the stitches go right through all the layers, but avoid stitching through the card.

8 Using pinking shears, cut out the heart shape from the aquamarine backing fabric. Cut close to the edge of the heart, but leave a narrow border and be careful not to cut through any stitches.

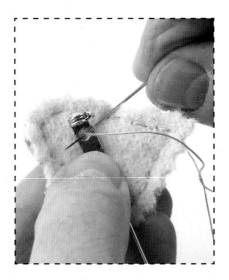

9 Stitch the brooch fastening to the back of the heart using any cotton thread. It is best to attach the fastening with the pin open as it makes it easier to get to the holes. Use a few stitches through each of the holes in the fastening to attach it securely.

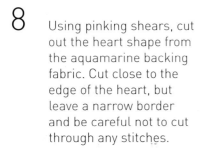

Brilliant Brooches

Brooches are great accessories to jazz up shirts, knitwear, hats, bags – or anything you can pin something to! The instructions show how to make the heart brooch, but you can also make flower ones, or even a bird.

Hanging Flower Heart

Hearts are popular shapes to make and give as gifts to loved ones. In the Folk Art of many countries, hearts have been used for centuries to decorate and embellish. They are a symbol of love and celebration and can be used to decorate textiles, furniture and other household items. This pretty pink heart is stitched with double knitting wool yarn for added strength, and has a plaited hanging loop so that it can be hung up easily. A lovely, simple project for the 'pink hearted'. Try replacing the stuffing with dried lavender for a fragrant gift to hang in your wardrobe or laundry cupboard.

YOU WILL NEED

Templates: Heart 2, Flower 3, Circle 1 and Circle 2

Felt in fuchsia pink, peach, turquoise and mauve

Thread: double knitting yarn in orange, turquoise, mauve and pink

Needles: sharp chenille or darning

Pins

Fabric scissors

Synthetic toy stuffing

1 Using the templates, cut out a large heart in pink felt and a peach flower. Position the peach flower in the centre of the pink heart and pin it in place. Thread a needle with orange double knitting yarn and bring it through to the front of the heart at the edge of the flower.

2   Overstitch the felt flower in place.

3   Using the template, cut out Circle 2 from turquoise felt and pin it to the centre of the peach flower. Secure the circle to the flower by overstitching around it using turquoise double knitting yarn.

4   Using the template, cut out Circle 1 from mauve felt, pin in place to the centre of the turquoise circle and then overstitch all around it using mauve double knitting yarn.

5   For some extra decoration, work running stitches around the outside of the turquoise circle on the peach felt using mauve double knitting yarn.

6   Using the template, cut out another large heart in pink felt and pin it to the back of the stitched heart. With pink double knitting yarn, use blanket stitch to close up the seam. Start about halfway along one side of the heart and remember to leave a gap for stuffing.

7 Stuff the heart using synthetic toy stuffing and then pin the seam together.

8 Blanket stitch the opening closed.

9 Make a plait using the same pink, orange and mauve double knitting yarn that has been used throughout. Make the plait 24cm (9½in) long and loop it in half.

10 Secure your looped plait to the heart by overstitching it to the 'dip' of the heart using pink double knitting yarn. Leave the tails of the different coloured yarns loose for added decoration.

Have My Heart

Hanging hearts are highly popular, contemporary items that make perfect gifts for weddings, christenings and Valentine's day. They can be hung from doors, dressers, wardrobes and drawers all around the home.

Bird Pincushion

Pincushions provide an ideal canvas for small-scale designs and are lovely little items to give away as gifts or to keep for oneself. To add interest, I thought it would be fun to start with a layered, diagonal background. The bird is made up of relatively small shapes. It is therefore a good way of using up scraps from other projects and provides plenty of scope to be imaginative with your colour schemes.

YOU WILL NEED

Templates: Square 1, Bird 2A–E and Circle 6

Felt in patterned and plain bright turquoise; patterned dark blue; and plain orange, royal blue, yellow, green and peach

Thread: purple satin thread; cotton perlé thread in turquoise, orange, yellow, green, blue, red and variegated orange/yellow; and cotton embroidery thread in coral pink and yellow

Needles: sharp chenille

Pins

Fabric scissors

Synthetic toy stuffing

1 Use the square template to cut out a large square in plain turquoise felt and a square section in patterned turquoise felt. Pin the patterned piece in position on the right side of the square and overstitch it in place using purple satin thread.

2 Using the template for the bird's body (Bird 2A), cut out the shape in patterned dark blue felt and pin it on to the centre of the square, overlapping both the plain and patterned sections. Overstitch all around the bird in turquoise cotton perlé thread.

3   Cut out the bird's head using the Bird 2E template in orange felt. Overstitch it in place on the left-hand end of the body using orange cotton perlé thread. Cut out the large wing in yellow using the template Bird 2B and overstitch it on to the body in yellow cotton perlé thread. Cut out the tail using the template Bird 2D in green and overstitch it to the right-hand end of the body using green cotton perlé thread.

4   Using the template Bird 2C, cut out the small wing in peach felt and overstitch it to the top edge of the body using a variegated orange/yellow cotton perlé thread.

5   Cut out a tiny circle for the eye in royal blue using the template Circle 6 and overstitch it in place on the bird's head using blue cotton perlé thread.

6   Using red cotton perlé thread, work some running stitches down the tail to decorate.

7   Couch on the legs (see page 14). Use coral pink embroidery thread for the laid thread and yellow embroidery thread for the couching stitches. Curve the legs slightly towards the tail end of the bird.

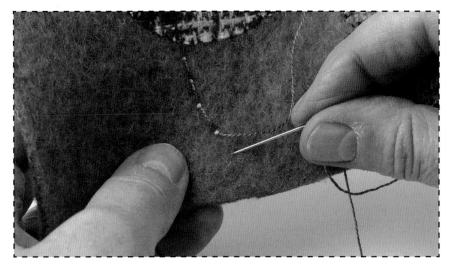

8 To make the feet, insert the needle threaded with the coral pink thread down into the fabric to make another stitch.

9 Bring the needle back up through the fabric, leaving a small gap between the new stitch and the end of last one. Insert it back down into the felt where the yellow couching ends.

10 Make another stitch on the other side to make three claws.

11 Repeat the process for the other leg and foot.

12 Cut out another large square from orange felt.

13 Sandwich the two squares together and blanket stitch all the way around the seam using cotton perlé thread in turquoise. Remember to leave a small space through which to insert the stuffing.

14 Stuff the pincushion firmly with synthetic toy stuffing.

15 Pin and stitch the seam closed using blanket stitch worked in turquoise cotton perlé thread.

Flower Pincushion

This project is great fun because it uses a mismatch of designs to create a crazy, busy effect. I used some patterned felt as well as a simple flower shape with random circles to fill up empty space. Use plain felt too, picking out some of the colours in the patterned felt to complement the colour scheme. This pincushion is another project where scraps of felt can be put to good use to create a totally random colour scheme. You could even go really wild and add small tassels or colourful pompoms in each corner.

YOU WILL NEED

Templates: Square 1, Flower 3, Circle 2, Circle 4 and Circle 6

Felt in terracotta orange, mauve and pale green; patterned green/orange and cream; and felt scraps in various complementing colours

Thread: cotton perlé thread in lime green, lilac, orange and variegated orange/yellow; and purple satin thread

Needles: sharp chenille

Pins

Fabric scissors

Synthetic toy stuffing

Stick a Pin in it

A fantastic pincushion is a great gift for someone who loves to sew. Get some fun, coloured pins to make them even brighter!

1 Using the template Square 1, cut out a large square of terracotta orange and a square section in patterned green/orange. Pin the two pieces together and overstitch in place using variegated orange/yellow thread.

2 Cut out a flower shape from the template Flower 3 in patterned cream felt and pin it in place in the centre of the square. Overstitch all the way around it using the variegated orange/yellow thread to secure it.

3 Cut out a circle using the Circle 2 template in mauve felt and overstitch it to the centre of the flower using purple satin thread.

4 Using the template Circle 4, cut out a small circle in pale green and overstitch it in place to the centre of the mauve circle with lime green cotton perlé thread.

5 Cut out about twelve tiny circles using the template Circle 6 in various colours that complement the project. Overstitch them randomly to the orange area of the pincushion, using lilac cotton perlé thread.

6 Cut out another orange square and lay your stitched orange square on top of it. Sew them together using blanket stitch and orange cotton perlé thread, leaving a gap for stuffing.

7 Stuff the pincushion with synthetic toy stuffing, pin the unstitched seam together and stitch it up using blanket stitch and orange cotton perlé thread.

Shield Bag

This little bag is a variation on the theme of crazy patchwork. Overlapping pieces of felt stitched with brightly coloured wool thread provide the background. A little bird, circles and a star placed randomly on top breaks up the surface. A colourful, plaited strap makes an easy and pretty finish.

YOU WILL NEED

Templates: Shield, Bird 3, Circle 1, Circle 4, Circle 5, Square 3 and Star 1

Cream base fabric (any fine, soft wool-based fabric will do)

Felt in red, green and various colours for the patchwork

Thread: machine/tacking thread; double knitting yarn in various colours; lime green cotton perlé thread

Needles: darning, sharp chenille

Pins

Fabric scissors

Embroidery scissors

Green bead for bird's eye

1 Using the template Shield, cut out the shield shape from the cream base fabric. Cut out each patchwork piece in a different coloured felt using the shapes on the shield template. Make sure you cut every piece slightly larger than the template shape to allow for some overlap.

2 Pin the different coloured pieces to the base fabric, using the template for guidance.

3 Overlap the pieces slightly as you pin them into position.

4 This shows the first top-left pieces overlapping and pinned to the base fabric.

5 Once all the pieces are pinned in position on the base fabric, use machine or tacking thread to tack all the pieces in place.

6 Your bag should now look like this.

7 Overstitch each section to the base fabric using double knitting yarn and a darning or chenille needle. Roughly match the yarn colour to the fabric colour or go for a different look by using contrasting colours.

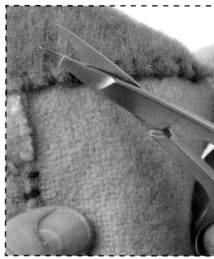

9 Once all of the sections have been overstitched in place, remove the tacking stitches by snipping them carefully with embroidery scissors.

8 Here, all the sections have been overstitched in place in matching or contrasting yarn.

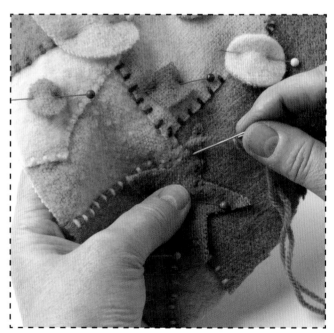

10 Cut out each of the other shapes using the remaining templates and pin them in place. I've cut out a tiny bird in pale pink, Circle 1 in yellow, Circle 4 in bright orange, two of Circle 5 in turquoise and in orange, Square 3 in red and Star 1 in bright pink.

11 Using a darning or chenille needle and matching or contrasting coloured double knitting yarn, overstitch around the edge of each of the little pinned-on shapes.

12 Cut out another two circles using the template Circle 5, one from blue felt and one from red felt. Overstitch the blue circle to the centre of the bright pink star using matching blue double knitting yarn, and overstitch the red circle to the top-right yellow circle using contrasting yarn.

13 Using lime green cotton perlé thread and a sharp chenille needle, stitch a green bead to the bird's head for an eye. Secure it in place with a few stitches.

14 Couch on the bird's legs. See page 14 for instructions on how to do this. Begin with the laid thread using double knitting yarn.

15 Use double knitting yarn in a contrasting colour to couch over the laid thread.

16 Make a three-clawed foot using three single stitches up to the couched thread leg. Repeat this process to make the other leg and foot.

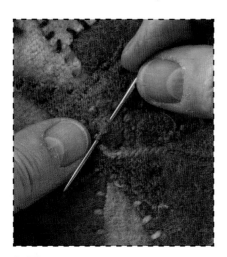

17 Make a French knot in the centre of each circle and at the points of the star using contrasting double knitting yarns.

18 Work two lines of running stitches around each circle to decorate using contrasting double knitting yarn.

19 On the right-hand purple section of the bag, randomly work some cross stitches using a matching double knitting thread.

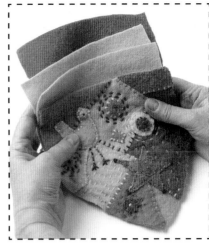

21 Cut out three more shield shapes; two in green and one in red. Sandwich them together with the red at the back, the green layers in the middle and the stitched layer face up on top. Pin them all together. You may have to trim the edges to achieve a neat edge.

20 On the left-hand turquoise area, use turquoise double knitting yarn to work random lines of running stitch in this area.

22 Using turquoise double knitting yarn, blanket stitch the layers together, ensuring you stitch right through all four layers. Leave the top of the bag open.

23 To create an opening for the bag, blanket stitch the front three layers together and then the back two layers together.

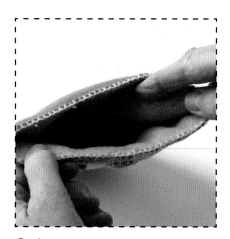

24 This will create a green lining for the bag.

25 Using a selection of the double knitting yarn colours you have used to make the bag, make a plait to a length of about 112cm (44in). Knot it at each end.

26 Stitch each end of the plait to one of the two top corners of the bag using a few overstitches and any coloured double knitting yarn. Leave the tails of knotted yarn free for decoration.

Pretty Purse

Use whatever colours and designs you fancy with this gorgeous bag. Give in to your creativity and make something really special and unique.

Bag Heaven

Like shoes, a girl can never have too many bags. These are made using a square instead of a shield template and a variety of motifs. To create the heart design, cut out two of each heart using the same size template but with contrasting colours, cut them in half, swap two halves of each and stitch them back together.

Cushion

A random selection of coloured squares form the background for this crazy patchwork cushion, and a simple pattern using petal shapes and circles is then sewn on top. The design is made specifically for a rectangular cushion, although it can be easily adapted to feature on quilts, bags, clothing or just about anything else!

YOU WILL NEED

Templates: Square 2, Leaf 2, Circle 1, Circle 2 and Circle 4

Felt in assorted colours of your choice and pale green felt for backing

Thread: white machine or tacking thread, and double knitting yarns in assorted colours of your choice

Needles: sharp chenille, darning

Pins

Fabric scissors

Cushion pad approximately 34 x 24cm (13½ x 9½in)

Sewing machine (optional)

1 Cut out 12 squares in an assortment of coloured felt, using the template Square 2. Pin all the squares together so that they slightly overlap each other to create a rectangle measuring 28.5 x 37.5cm (11¼ x 14¾in).

2 Using machine or tacking thread, tack the pinned squares together.

3 Overstitch the squares along the edges in complementary or contrasting double knitting yarn, using a different colour for each square.

4 Using the leaf and circle templates, cut out a variety of different sized circles and leaves/ petals in assorted colours of felt. Pin the motifs in place following the design below, making sure the colours work with the squares that they are pinned to.

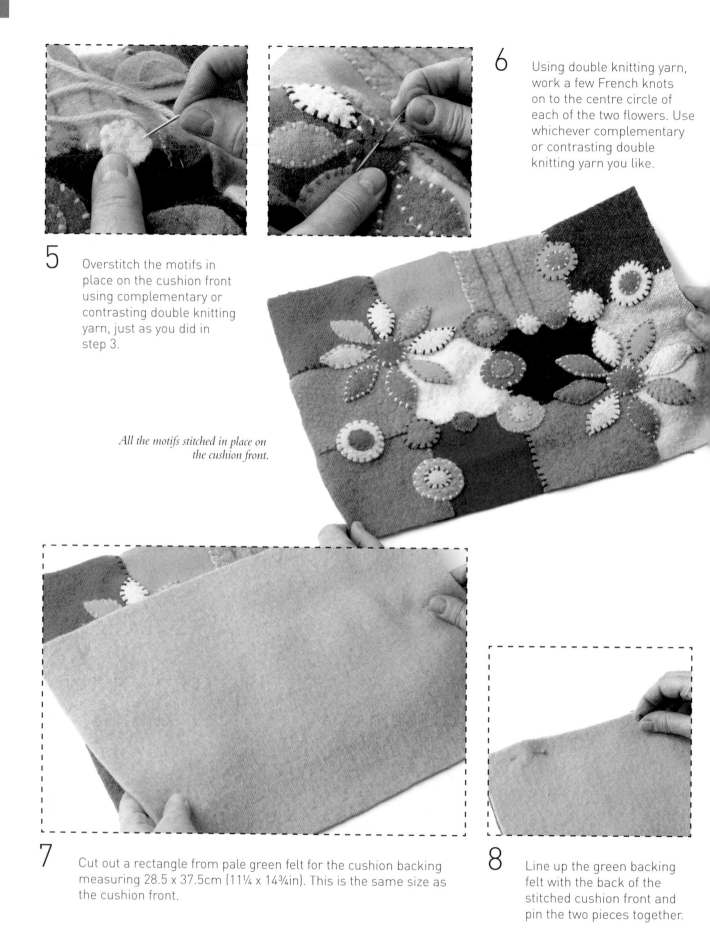

6 Using double knitting yarn, work a few French knots on to the centre circle of each of the two flowers. Use whichever complementary or contrasting double knitting yarn you like.

5 Overstitch the motifs in place on the cushion front using complementary or contrasting double knitting yarn, just as you did in step 3.

All the motifs stitched in place on the cushion front.

7 Cut out a rectangle from pale green felt for the cushion backing measuring 28.5 x 37.5cm (11¼ x 14¾in). This is the same size as the cushion front.

8 Line up the green backing felt with the back of the stitched cushion front and pin the two pieces together.

9 Machine stitch three sides of the cushion together, with wrong sides facing, approximately 1cm (½in) from the fabric edge, leaving one short side open to insert the cushion pad. Use whichever colour machine thread you like for this. You can also hand stitch this step if you prefer, or use a blanket stitch in a complementary colour.

10 Once stitched, turn the cushion cover the right way out.

11 Carefully insert a rectangular cushion pad into the unstitched, open end of the cover.

12 With the cushion pad inserted, turn the open seam in by 1cm (½in) all the way around and pin it together.

13 Using machine thread, overstitch the seam closed. Make evenly spaced, small stitches for a neat finish.

This cushion will add a splash of colour to any bedroom or living area. An ideal gift for that one special person who enjoys relaxing on the sofa a little too much ...

Simply Square

Why not have a go at making these cushions too? They're made in the same way, but are square shaped and use different motifs and different colours.

Four Seasons Wall Hanging

While developing this project it was very interesting and somewhat challenging to work out which colours to use to successfully convey the differences between the four seasons. Eventually I decided to use lime green and pastels for the fresh awakening of spring, stronger, warm colours for summer, the countryside aglow with bracken and ripened fruit and mists for autumn, and the crisp snow and red berries of winter. The four little houses have been designed to stand on their own or to work as a group to convey the changing seasons throughout the year. Feel free to add details such as trees or animals to create the perfect 'Welcome to Your New Home' gift. The steps below show you how to make the summer wall hanging.

YOU WILL NEED

Templates: Hill 1, Hill 2, Square 4, Roof, Door, Window, Chimney, Corner 1, Corner 2, Border 1, Border 2, Leaf 3, Circle 5 and Circle 6

Cream base fabric (any fine, soft wool-based fabric will do)

Felt in turquoise, pale green, lime green, bright pink, yellow, orange and pale yellow

Thread: cotton perlé thread in pale green, lime green, bright pink, yellow, orange and turquoise; and silk thread in bright pink

Needles: sharp embroidery

Pins

Fabric scissors

Curtain ring

1 Cut out two squares, each measuring 20cm (7¾in) square, one in turquoise felt and one in a cream base fabric. For this base, I used old blanket fabric but any soft fabric that your needle will go through easily will do. Pin the two squares together.

2 Using the template, cut out the hill shape using Hill 1 from pale green felt and pin it to the bottom of the turquoise square. Overstitch around the top of the hill to hold it in place using pale green cotton perlé thread and a sharp embroidery needle.

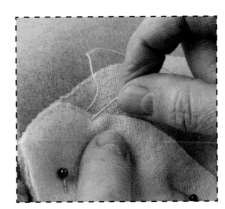

3 Cut out the second hill shape from lime green felt using the template Hill 2. Pin it to the left side of the pale green hill. Overstitch the second hill in place using lime green cotton perlé thread and a sharp embroidery needle.

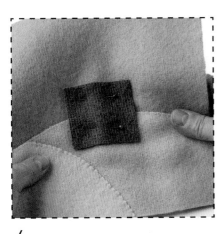

4 Using the template Square 4, cut out a square for the house from bright pink felt and position it in the centre of the picture. Pin it in place.

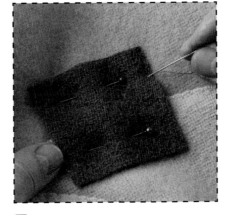

5 Overstitch around three sides of the house using bright pink cotton perlé thread to secure it in place. Leave the top edge unstitched.

6 Cut out the roof using the roof template in yellow felt and position it on top of the pink house, slightly overlapping the top unstitched edge of the square. Using yellow cotton perlé thread, overstitch all the way around the edge of the roof.

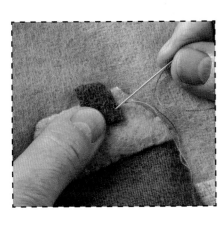

7 Cut out the chimney shape from orange felt using the appropriate template and overstitch it in place on top of the roof using orange cotton perlé thread and a sharp embroidery needle.

8 Using the window template, cut out four pale green windows and position them on the house, leaving space for the door. Overstitch around each one in pale green cotton perlé.

9 Cut out and position the turquoise front door on the left of the house and overstitch around the edge using turquoise cotton perlé thread.

10 Cut out a tiny orange circle for the window of the front door using the Circle 6 template. Position it in the centre of the door and overstitch it all around in orange cotton perlé thread to secure.

11 To stitch the fence, use pale green cotton perlé thread to make five vertical straight stitches on either side of the house on top of the hill. Do not fasten off the thread.

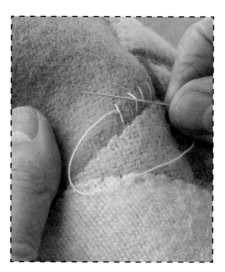

12 Bring your needle back through to the front of the fabric halfway along the last fence post you stitched. Loop it around the next fence post along.

13 Pull the thread taut and then repeat this technique along the rest of the stitches to make the fence.

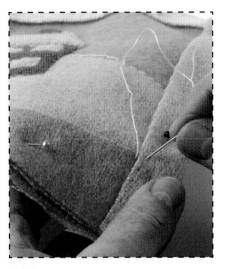

14 Cut out the border using two of Border 1 and two of Border 2. Use lime green, pale yellow, pale green and turquoise felt. Pin the two horizontal pieces in place, followed by the two verticals.

15 Overstitch the inside edge of the frame only and use matching cotton perlé thread.

16 Using the template Corner 1, cut out two small rectangles in bright pink for the top-left and bottom-right corners. For the other corners, cut two small squares using the template Corner 2 in bright pink. Pin and then overstitch them securely using bright pink cotton perlé thread.

17 Cut out five leaves in lime green and five in pale green using the template Leaf 3. Also cut five of Circle 5 in orange. Overstitch the leaves on to the scene using lime green and pale green cotton perlé thread. See the image of the finished hanging on page 61 for the exact positioning of the leaves.

18 Overstitch the orange circles in place, overlapping the green leaves. Use orange cotton perlé thread.

19 Work some running stitches down each leaf in matching green thread to show the veins.

20 Using silk thread in bright pink, work a star stitch in the centre of each of the orange circles for added decoration.

21 Using lime green cotton perlé thread, work some random star stitches on to the main pale green hill. Work some random lines of running stitches across the lime green hill.

22 Work some parallel rows of running stitches on to the turquoise background using turquoise cotton perlé thread. Work in a curving, flowing manner across the sky.

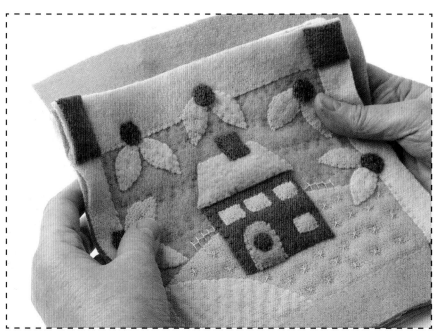

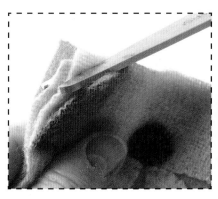

24 To stop the corners becoming too bulky, trim off the middle layers of fabric with fabric scissors. Pin all the layers together and, using the pale green cotton perlé thread, blanket stitch all the way around the outside edge, through all the layers.

23 Cut out the backing square from turquoise felt and trim the stitched square and the backing square so they fit neatly together.

25 Stitch a curtain ring to the back of the piece in order to hang it, following the instructions on page 18.

All Year Round

The step-by-step instructions show you how to make the summer wall hanging. However, by using the same templates but different colours, you can make a decoration for every season. Use pastel colours for spring, strong colours for summer, rich colours for autumn and, of course, lots of white for winter.

Festive Star

Here is a bright, sparkling star to decorate
your home for a special festival or celebration.
Stars symbolise hope shining in the darkness,
so what could be better than making one of
your very own to give cheer during the twelve
days of Christmas or the long, dark days of the
winter months?

YOU WILL NEED

Templates: Star 1, Star 2,
  Circle 5, Circle 7, Circle 8,
  Triangle 1 and Triangle 2

Felt in turquoise, bright pink,
  orange, yellow and blue

Thread: cotton perlé thread
  in pink, orange, yellow,
  turquoise and green; satin
  thread in orange; and silk
  thread in bright pink

Needles: sharp chenille

Pins

Fabric scissors

Bright pink sequins

Thin card

Scraps of silk and cotton
  multicoloured fabrics

Curtain ring

1 Cut out a rectangle of
turquoise felt approximately
24 x 28cm (9½ x 11in). Then,
using the template Star 2,
cut out a large star from
bright pink felt and pin it
roughly to the centre of
the turquoise felt. Using
pink cotton perlé thread,
overstitch all around the
star to secure it in place.

2 Using the template Circle
7, cut out a circle in orange
felt and overstitch it in place
to the centre of the pink star
using orange cotton perlé
thread.

3   Cut out a small star using template Star 1 in yellow felt and position it in the centre of the orange circle. Overstitch it in place all around the edges in yellow cotton perlé thread.

4   Cut out a tiny circle using template Circle 5 in blue felt and position it in the centre of the yellow star. Overstitch it in place using turquoise cotton perlé thread.

5   Cut out four small triangles using the template Triangle 2 in blue felt and overstitch them in place with turquoise cotton perlé thread to the top-left and -right and the bottom-left and -right points of the star.

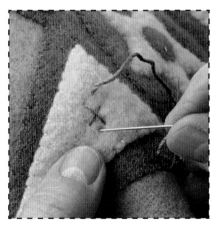

6   Using green cotton perlé thread, make three groups of three straight stitches on each of the blue triangles, as shown above. These are constructed in the same way as the bird's feet in the Shield Bag project on page 46.

7   Cut out two large triangles using the template Triangle 1 in yellow felt and overstitch them to the two largest pink star points using yellow cotton perlé thread.

8   Using orange satin thread, work a star stitch on to each of the yellow triangles.

9 Work three star stitches in orange satin thread on each of the two remaining small pink star points. Work these stitches in decreasing size, from the point to the centre of the star.

10 Attach a bright pink sequin to the centre of the tiny blue circle on the small yellow star. Use bright pink cotton perlé thread.

11 Attach a line of bright pink sequins all the way around the orange circle, keeping them all an equal distance apart.

12 Cut out four yellow circles using the template Circle 8 and, using overstitch, secure them to the four points of the star that have the blue triangles sewn on to them. Make sure they overlap the ends of the points slightly and use yellow cotton perlé thread.

13 Using bright pink silk thread, work a star stitch on each of the four yellow circles on the four points of the star.

14 Carefully cut out the star from the turquoise fabric using fabric scissors. Leave a narrow border, and be careful not to cut through any of the stitching.

15 Cut out a card star that is slightly smaller than the felt star using template Star 2. Take another rectangle of turquoise felt, approximately the same size as that in step 1. Sandwich the card star between the turquoise felt rectangle and the stitched star and pin all the layers together.

16 Using turquoise cotton perlé thread and running stitch, attach the stitched star to the turquoise rectangle, with the card in between. Stitch all the way around the edge, making sure you go through both layers of felt. Do not stitch through the card.

17 Carefully cut out the fabric star from the turquoise rectangle as in step 14, avoiding cutting into the running stitches.

18 Cut random strips of multicoloured silk and cotton fabrics, approximately 0.5cm (¼in) wide and 6cm (2¼in) long.

19 Gather the strips together, fold them in half and knot them together in the middle.

20 Trim the strips to size. Make three more tassels in the same way.

21 Rub and pull at the tassels to fray them slightly for added texture. Use overstitch or stab stitches and pink cotton perlé thread to attach the fabric tassels to the four points of the star without circles.

22 The completed star should look like this.

23 Attach a curtain ring to the back of the star for hanging, following the instructions on page 18.

Bright Star

This star would be bright enough to guide three wise men across the desert, but would look even better sitting on top of your tree!

Tree Top Bird

Christmas is always a lovely time for decorations, and this bird will look very pretty on top of the tree. A simple colour scheme has been used here, with silver sequins and wire adding subtle festive sparkle. If you prefer, why not stitch the bird motif on to a cushion, or add a loop and have it keeping watch out of the window?

YOU WILL NEED

- Templates: Bird 4A–C, Snowflake 1, Circle 1, Circle 9 and Square 5
- Felt in cream, red, pale green and turquoise
- Thread: cotton perlé thread in red, turquoise, white and pale green; and white cotton sewing thread
- Needles: sharp chenille
- Pins
- Fabric scissors
- Small white pearl button
- Five silver leaf sequins
- Silver spangles
- Craft wire
- Thin card
- Curtain ring

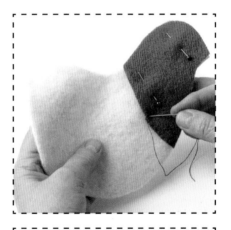

1 Using the templates, cut out three bird shapes: the head in red (Bird 4C), the body in cream (Bird 4A) and the tail in pale green (Bird 4B). Pin the head to the head-end of the body. Overstitch it in place using red cotton perlé thread along the inside edge only.

2 Cut out a small turquoise circle for the eye using template Circle 1 and pin it in place on the bird's head. Overstitch all the way around the eye using turquoise cotton perlé thread.

3 Attach a small white pearl button to the centre of the circle and secure it in place with a few stitches using white cotton perlé thread.

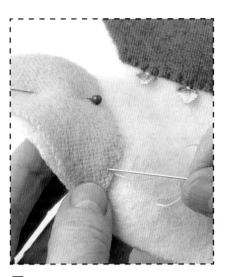

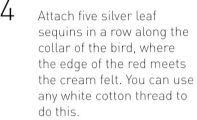

4   Attach five silver leaf sequins in a row along the collar of the bird, where the edge of the red meets the cream felt. You can use any white cotton thread to do this.

5   Pin the tail in position over the tail end of the bird. Overstitch it in place along the inside edge only using pale green cotton perlé thread.

6   Using the template Snowflake 1, cut out a snowflake from turquoise felt and pin it in place near the centre of the bird's body. Overstitch all the way around the snowflake in turquoise cotton perlé thread.

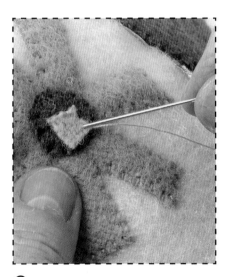

7   Cut out a tiny circle in red felt using the Circle 9 template and position it in the centre of the snowflake. Overstitch it in place using red cotton perlé thread.

8   Cut out a tiny pale green square using the template Square 5 and position it at a slight angle in the centre of the red circle. Stitch it in place using overstitches and pale green cotton perlé thread.

9   Stitch a sprinkling of silver spangles on to the red area of the bird's head using any white cotton thread.

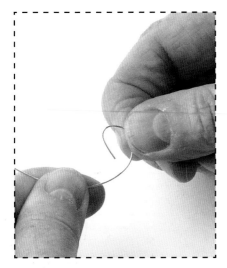

10 To make the tail feathers, take a length of craft wire approximately 17cm (6¾in) long and bend it round into a coil at one end.

11 Turn up the other end of the wire into a loop to allow you to stitch it in place more easily. Make another two tail feathers in the same way.

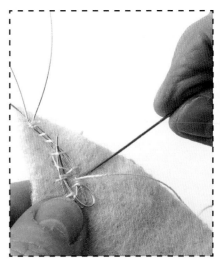

12 Overstitch the three wire loops to the back of the tail-end of the bird to secure. Use white cotton thread and stitch through the cream felt layer only so that no stitches show on the green tail on the front.

13 Cut out a bird shape in cream felt using the stitched bird as a template. Also cut out a card bird shape which is slightly smaller than the stitched bird. Sandwich the card bird between the two felt birds and pin all the layers together.

14 Stitch all the way around the outside edge of the bird using white cotton perlé thread and blanket stitch. Stitch right through all the layers to secure everything together. Avoid stitching through the card.

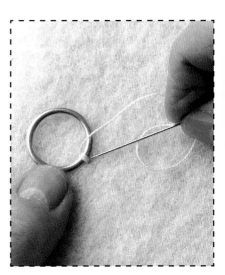

15 Attach a curtain ring to the back of the bird for hanging following the instructions on page 18.

Dove of Peace

Give this bird a home by nesting it at the top of your Christmas tree this year - a fun alternative to the traditional star decoration.

Garland of Angels

The inspiration for the Garland of Angels came from the folded string of paper cut-outs we all used to make as children. This row of angelic figures is perfect to hang above a mantelpiece or dresser. Make as many angels as you want in a variety of colourways and join them together following the instructions below. An alternative design is also provided for a larger, more intricately embellished angel that can be displayed on its own.

YOU WILL NEED

Templates: Skirt, Hem, Arm, Waistband, Bodice, Angel's Wing, Hair 1, Circle 4, Circle 10 and Snowflake 2

Felt in pale green, turquoise, red, white and yellow

Thread: cotton perlé thread in turquoise, red, white, yellow, dark blue and pale green; and thick yellow cotton thread

Needles: sharp chenille

Pins

Fabric scissors

Small white pearl buttons

Red colouring pencil

Small silver sequins

Bondaweb

Iron

Turquoise acrylic backing fabric

Curtain rings

1 Using the appropriate templates, cut out the skirt shape from pale green felt and the hem of the skirt from turquoise felt. Pin the hem to the bottom of the skirt and overstitch it in place along the inside edge only with turquoise cotton perlé thread.

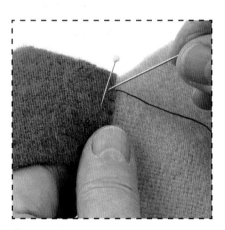

2 Cut out the red bodice and pin it to the top of the skirt. Overstitch it in place using red cotton perlé thread.

3 Cut out the turquoise waistband and pin it in place where the bodice and the skirt meet. Overstitch it in place using turquoise cotton perlé thread.

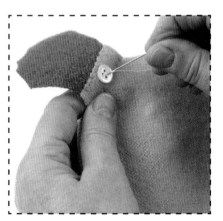

4 Sew a white pearl button to the centre of the waistband using white cotton perlé thread. Use a few small stitches to secure it in place.

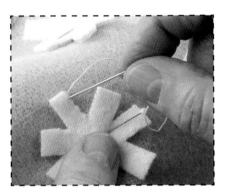

5   Cut out three snowflakes from white felt using the template Snowflake 2 and pin them on to the skirt. Stitch around each white snowflake using overstitch and white cotton perlé thread.

6   Cut out three tiny circles in red felt using template Circle 10 and overstitch them to the centre of each snowflake using red cotton perlé thread.

7   Using the Angel's Wings template, cut out the wings in white felt and pin them in position on the back of the red bodice. Overstitch the wings in place using red cotton perlé thread.

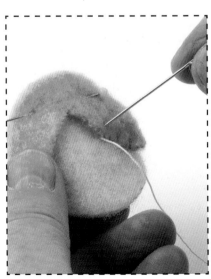

8   For the head, cut out a white circle using the template Circle 4 and cut out the hair shape from yellow felt using the template Hair 1. Pin the hair to the head and overstitch in place using yellow cotton perlé thread.

9   Work a number of French knots (see page 15) on to the hair in a thick yellow cotton thread.

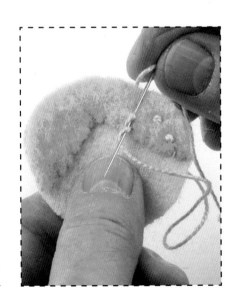

10 Work two French knots in dark blue thread on the face for the angel's eyes. Make a few tiny straight stitches in a line for the mouth using red cotton perlé thread.

11 Using an ordinary red colouring pencil, draw two tiny dots on either side of the mouth to make the cheeks.

12 Pin the head in position on to the body, slightly overlapping the bodice and the wings. Overstitch the head in place using white cotton perlé thread, taking care to go through all the layers of felt.

13 Cut out two arms from white felt and pin one on each side of the bodice. The end of each arm should be about 8.5cm (3¼in) in length when sewn on so that, when the angels are attached to each other, they can hold hands comfortably without distorting the shape of the garland. Overstitch the arms to the bodice using red cotton perlé thread.

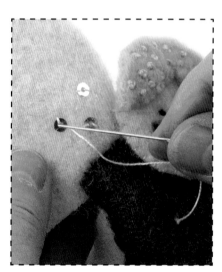

14 Attach a sprinkling of silver sequins to the angel's wings using any white cotton thread and a few small stitches.

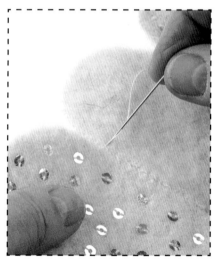

15 Make several angels, varying the colours and embellishments used. Using overstitch and any white cotton thread, lay the angels side by side in a row and sew the wings together where they touch using overstitch.

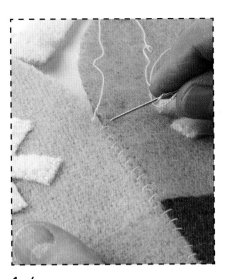

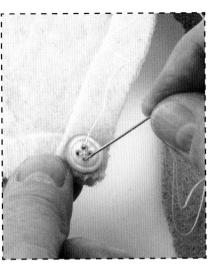

16 Line up the bottoms of the skirts as a guide and use pale green cotton perlé thread to overstitch them together.

17 Join the hands together by overlapping one on top of the other and sewing on a white pearl button where they overlap.

18 Once all your angels have been sewn together, turn them over and iron some Bondaweb on to the back of them.

19 Carefully cut out your garland of angels from the Bondaweb.

20 Pin the garland to a piece of turquoise acrylic backing fabric big enough for the entire garland to fit on to.

21 Carefully cut out the garland of angels from the acrylic backing fabric.

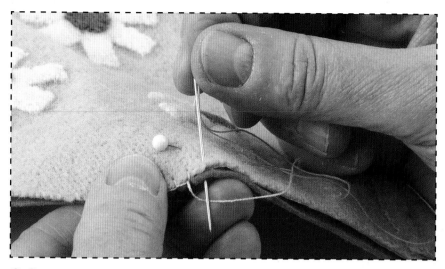 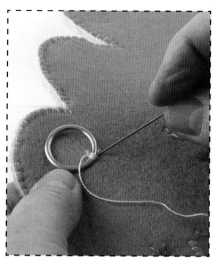

22 Join all the layers of pinned fabric together by blanket stitching all the way around the whole garland in pale green cotton perlé thread.

23 Attach a curtain ring to the back of the head of each angel for hanging.

Hark the Herald Angels Sing!

This garland of angels is a perfect decoration for a little girl's wardrobe, or to hang above the bed to keep watch at night time!

Angel

This beautiful angel is slightly larger than those in the garland, and is more intricately decorated. Use the angel template enlarged by 150%, and cut out the felt motifs using the templates Flower 4, Circle 5 and Wing 1.

The Princess and the Pea

A pretty project for a little girl's room, inspired by the well-loved fairy story with mattresses piled high, a beautiful princess and a small green pea. This timeless tale worked in felt and thread will capture the imagination and enhance any little princess's room. I enjoyed using a mixture of tweeds and strips of material to represent the mattresses and I added some gold and silver threads for a touch of magic.

YOU WILL NEED

- Templates: Bed A–F, Pillow, Hair 2, Head, Heart 1, Circle 2, Circle 5, Circle 8, Mattress 1–8
- Felt in cream, bright pink, turquoise, lime green, pink-beige and yellow; and patterned felt and tweed woollen fabric in pale blues, creams and greys
- Thread: white and black machine or tacking thread; satin thread in bright pink, turquoise and orange; cotton perlé thread in white, pale blue, lime green, yellow, red and mauve; thick cotton perlé thread in white and yellow; and silver and gold lurex thread
- Needles: sharp chenille
- Pins
- Fabric scissors
- Two silver sequins
- Thin card
- Two curtain rings

1 Cut out a piece of cream felt 31 x 48cm (12¼ x 19in) and, using the template Bed C, cut out the long section of the bedstead in bright pink felt. Pin it to the left-hand side of the cream fabric. Use bright pink satin thread to overstitch the bedstead strip in place all the way around the edge.

2 Cut out all the mattress pieces and pin them in place in the same order as the templates, with the left-hand edges against the right-hand edge of the pink strip. Use patterned felt and/or patterned tweed fabrics in pale blues, creams and greys to create the desired effect. Tack them in place using machine or tacking thread. Cut out the right-hand bed leg using the template Bed D from the bright pink felt and tuck it under the bottom mattress on the right-hand side, pinning it in place.

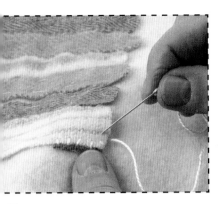

3 Overstitch around each mattress piece using thick white cotton perlé thread for the cream/white mattress pieces, and pale blue cotton perlé thread for the blue mattress pieces.

4 Add some decorative stitches to the mattresses in silver lurex thread and turquoise, orange and bright pink satin thread. Use running stitches and straight stitches worked in zigzags.

5 To make each bed wheel, cut out a small turquoise circle using template Circle 8 and a tiny bright pink circle using Circle 2. Overstitch the pink circle to the centre of the turquoise circle using bright pink satin thread. Using thick white cotton perlé thread, work a line of running stitches around the small circle.

6 Using turquoise satin thread, work a star stitch into the centre of the pink circle. Repeat steps 5 and 6 to make the other bed wheel.

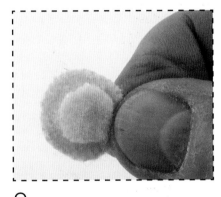

7 Pin each wheel in place, slightly overlapping the bottom of the bed legs. Overstitch around each wheel in the same bright turquoise thread.

8 To make the pea, cut out a tiny lime green circle using the template Circle 5 and a slightly smaller circle in cream. Lay the smaller circle, centred, on top of the green circle. Flip it over so that the green circle is facing upwards and position it in the curved gap between the lower two mattresses. The smaller circle acts as a padding, giving the pea a rounded appearance.

9 Overstitch all around the pea in lime green cotton perlé thread.

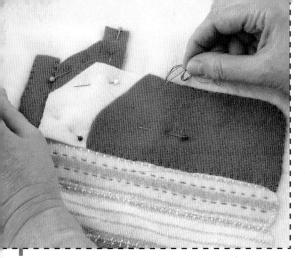

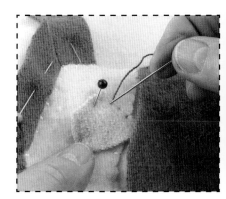

10 Using the templates Bed A, Bed B and Bed E, cut out the component parts of the top of the bed in bright pink felt. Cut out the pillow from cream felt. Pin the different sections in place, using the picture as a guide. Using bright pink satin thread, overstitch around the bed cover, leaving the top open for the princess's head.

11 Overstitch around the pillow using thick white cotton perlé thread.

12 Cut out the head shape in pink-beige felt and tuck the neck end just under the pink cover. Pin it in place. Overstitch down the sides of the head using bright pink satin thread. The hair will cover the rest of the head and will secure it in place.

13 Cut out the sheet section of the bed cover in cream felt and pin it to the bed so that it overlaps the cover and the head slightly. Overstitch it in place using thick white cotton perlé thread.

14 Cut out a cream rectangle using the template Bed F. Over-stitch it in place on the left-hand section of the bedstead, level with the top of Mattress 1, using thick white cotton perlé thread.

15 Cut out the hair from yellow felt and pin it in place, overlapping the head. Use thick yellow cotton perlé thread to overstitch the hair in place all the way around.

16 Using silver lurex thread, stitch one row of tiny running stitches across the top sheet for added decoration.

17 For the face, stitch on the eyebrows and the nose in stem stitch using black machine thread.

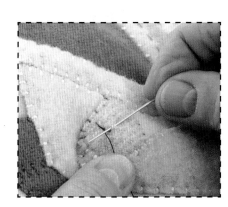

18 Stitch on the eyes by making a 'V' shape with a stitch across it, like an upside down 'A'. For the lips, stitch on a few straight stitches side by side in red cotton perlé thread underneath the nose.

19 To add texture to the hair, work running stitches in parallel lines down the length of it in yellow cotton perlé thread. Repeat using gold lurex thread.

20 Secure two silver sequins on to the top of the hair using silver lurex thread.

21 Using the templates Heart 1 and Circle 5, cut out a small heart in turquoise felt and a tiny cream circle. Overstitch the circle on to the centre of the heart in thick white cotton perlé thread.

22 Using bright pink satin thread, embroider a star stitch on to the centre of the cream circle. Make another heart in the same way.

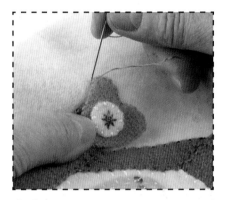

23 Pin the hearts to the top of the bedposts, slightly overlapping them. Overstitch them in place using turquoise satin thread.

24 Using mauve cotton perlé thread, work tiny cross stitches all the way across the pink cover for added decoration.

25 Using thick white cotton perlé thread, work a line of fly stitches (touching) vertically down each bedpost (see page 14).

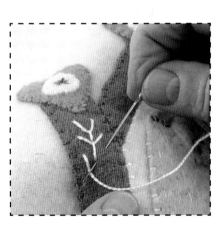

26 Carefully cut out the stitched bed from the cream backing felt using fabric scissors.

27 Cut out some card slightly smaller than the bed shape. Cut out another rectangle of cream felt, the same size as the one in step 1. Sandwich the card between the cream rectangle and the back of the stitched bed and pin together.

28 Using white cotton perlé thread, stitch through the layers of fabric with running stitches all the way around the bed. Avoid stitching through the card in between.

29 Carefully cut out the bed from the cream felt, taking care that all the edges are level with one another. Avoid cutting through any of the stitches.

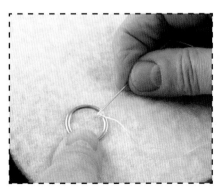

30 Attach two curtain rings to the back of the stitched piece, one on each side at the top, for hanging it on to the wall.

Sleeping Beauty

Encourage lots of sweet dreams with this wall hanging that is fit for royalty!

Snowflakes

These simple, contemporary decorations use a traditional and limited colour scheme and are useful to make if you want to use up scraps of felt.

YOU WILL NEED

Templates: Snowflake 2, Circle 11, Circle 8 and Square 5

Felt in white, red and pale green

Thread: cotton perlé thread in red, pale green and white; and white cotton sewing thread

Needles: sharp chenille

Pins

Fabric scissors

Silver spangle

Cotton string

Thin card

Festive Flakes

Decorating the tree at Christmas time is always a fun family activity – make it extra special this year by adding your own personal touch with these beautiful snowflake decorations.

1 Cut out a circle using template Circle 11 in white felt and a snowflake shape in red felt. Pin the snowflake to the centre of the white circle and overstitch it in place all the way around using red cotton perlé thread.

2 Cut out a tiny pale green circle using the template Circle 8 and attach it to the centre of the red snowflake. Overstitch all the way around it in pale green cotton perlé thread.

3 Cut out a tiny square in white felt using the template Square 5 and position it in the centre of the pale green circle. Overstitch it in place all the way around in white cotton perlé thread.

4 Attach a silver spangle to the centre of the tiny white square with a few stitches worked in white cotton thread.

5 Take a length of cotton string, approximately 25cm (9¾in) long, fold it in half and knot the ends together to form a loop. Stitch the loop in place on the back of the stitched white circle using a few overstitches and white cotton thread.

6 Cut out a circle of card slightly smaller than the stitched felt circle and another circle in white felt the same size as the stitched circle.

7 Sandwich the card between the plain white circle and the back of the stitched circle and pin the layers together.

8 Using white cotton perlé thread, blanket stitch all the way around the sandwiched circles through both layers to join them, avoiding stitching through the card. Remove any pins.

Hanging Hearts

These adorable hanging hearts are a great alternative to the snowflake decorations - and can be used all year round to brighten up your home! Here they have been made up in patriotic red, white and blue, but feel free to experiment with new combinations of colours.

Templates

All the templates are provided at the size they are to be used for the projects in this book. Simply photocopy or trace them, cut them out, pin them to your piece of felt and cut around the edge. You can store your templates in a folder for future use, but make sure the name of the template is written on if necessary.

On the following pages, I have tried to group the templates according to project. However, some of the templates are used more than once and in these cases they are provided with the first project in which they are used.

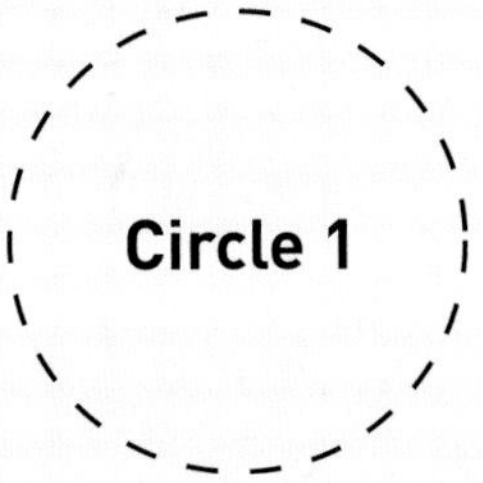

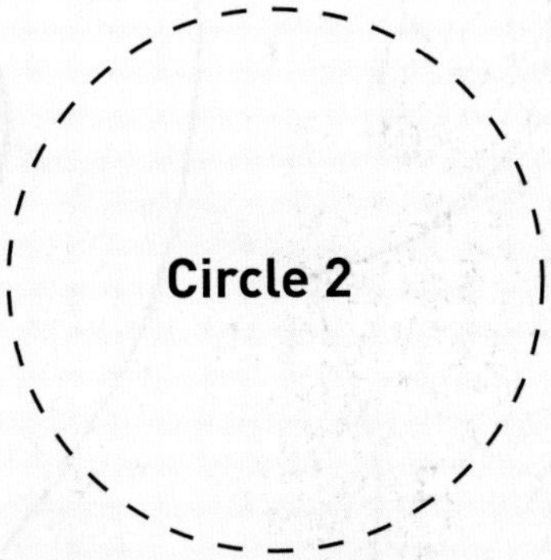

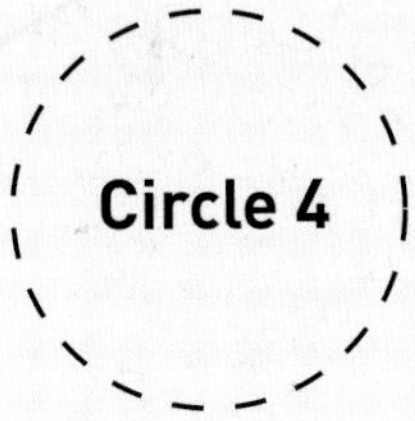

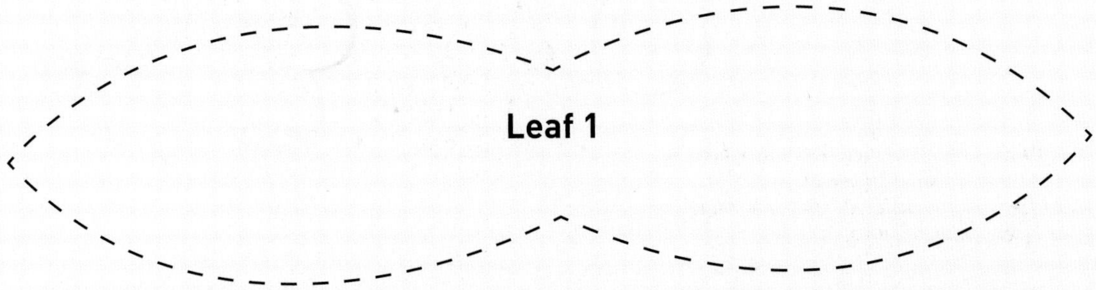

Circle 1

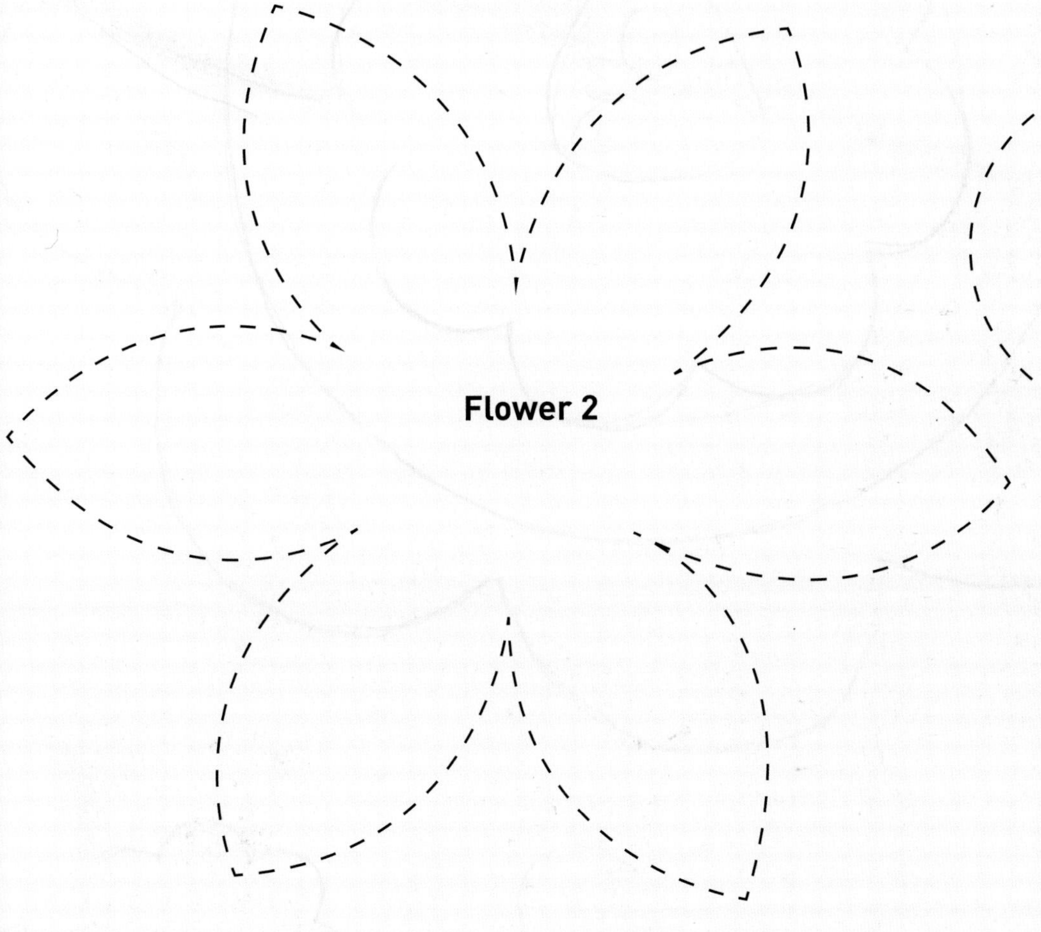

Circle 2

Flower 2

Circle 4

Leaf 1

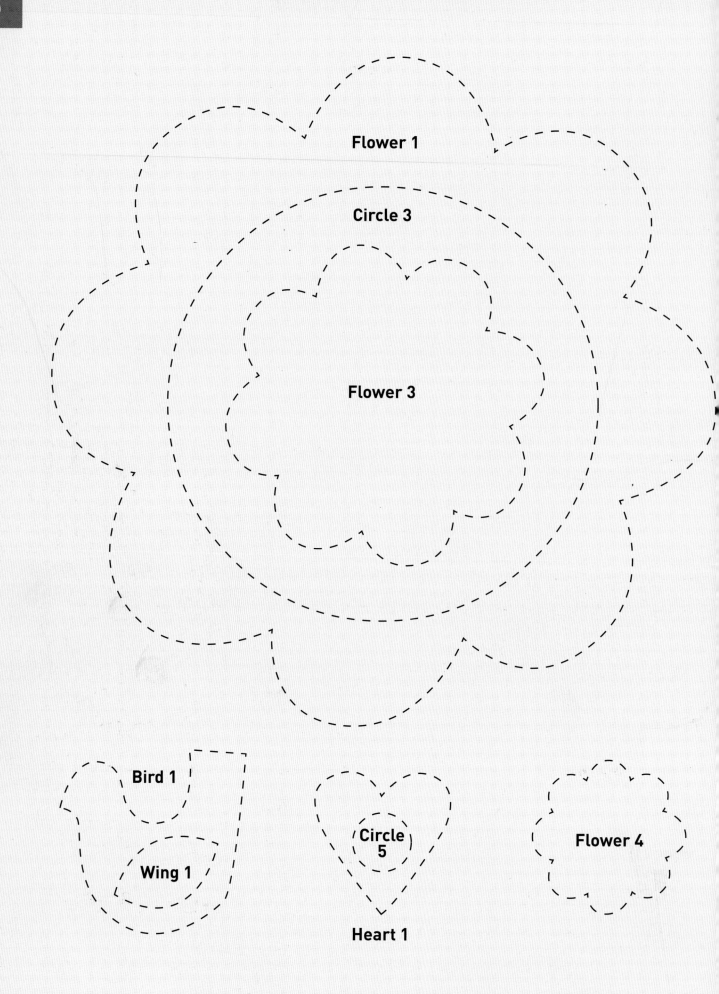

Flower 1

Circle 3

Flower 3

Bird 1

Wing 1

Circle 5

Flower 4

Heart 1

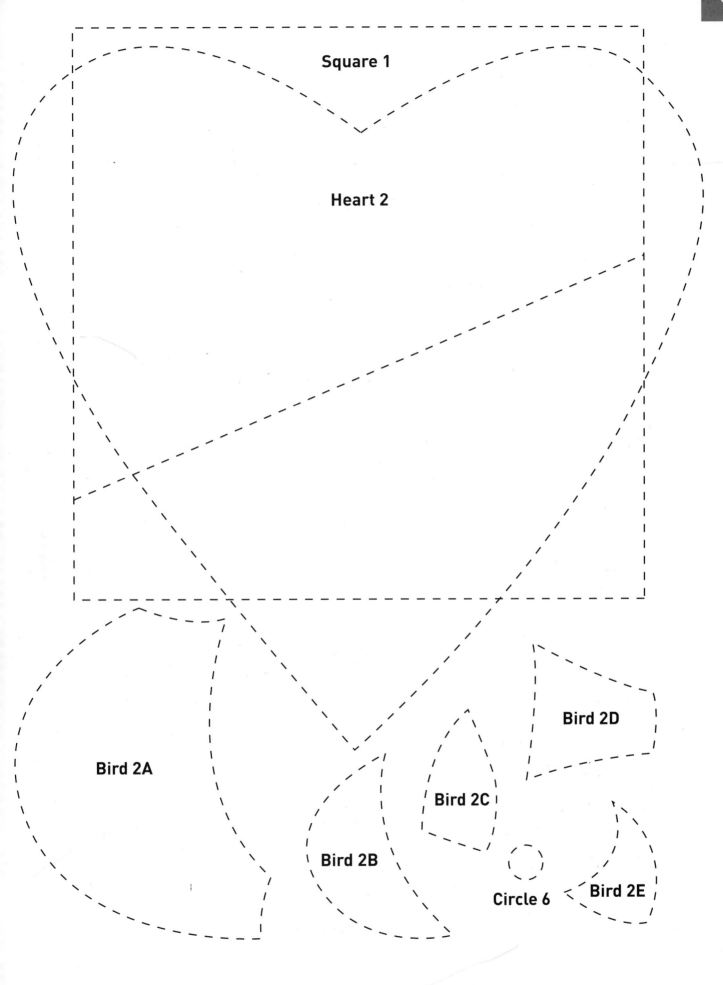

Square 1

Heart 2

Bird 2A

Bird 2B

Bird 2C

Bird 2D

Bird 2E

Circle 6

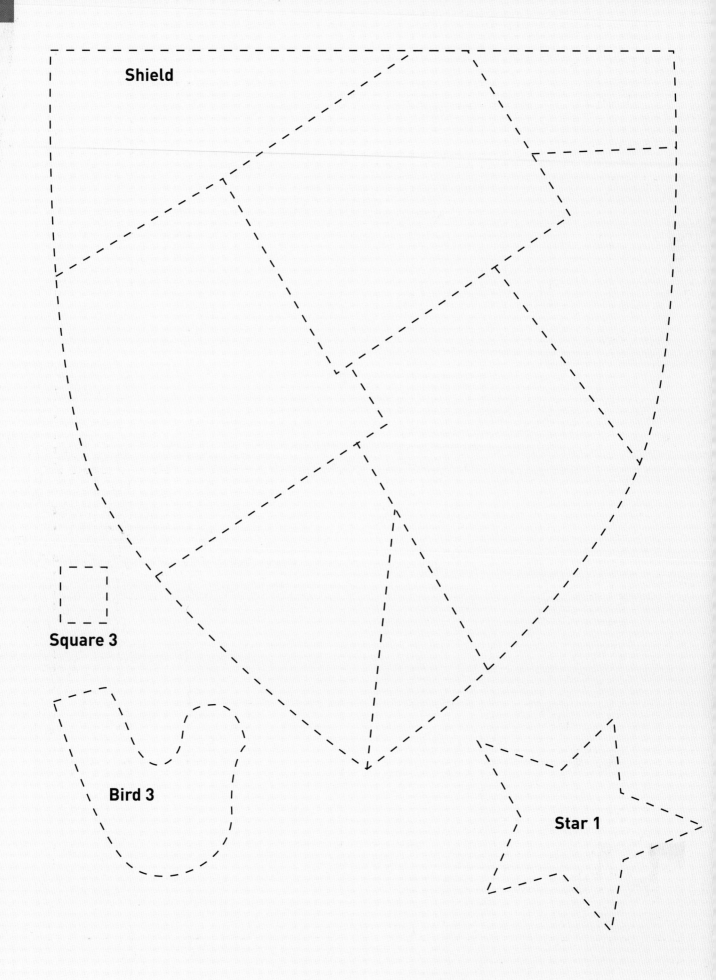

Shield

Square 3

Bird 3

Star 1

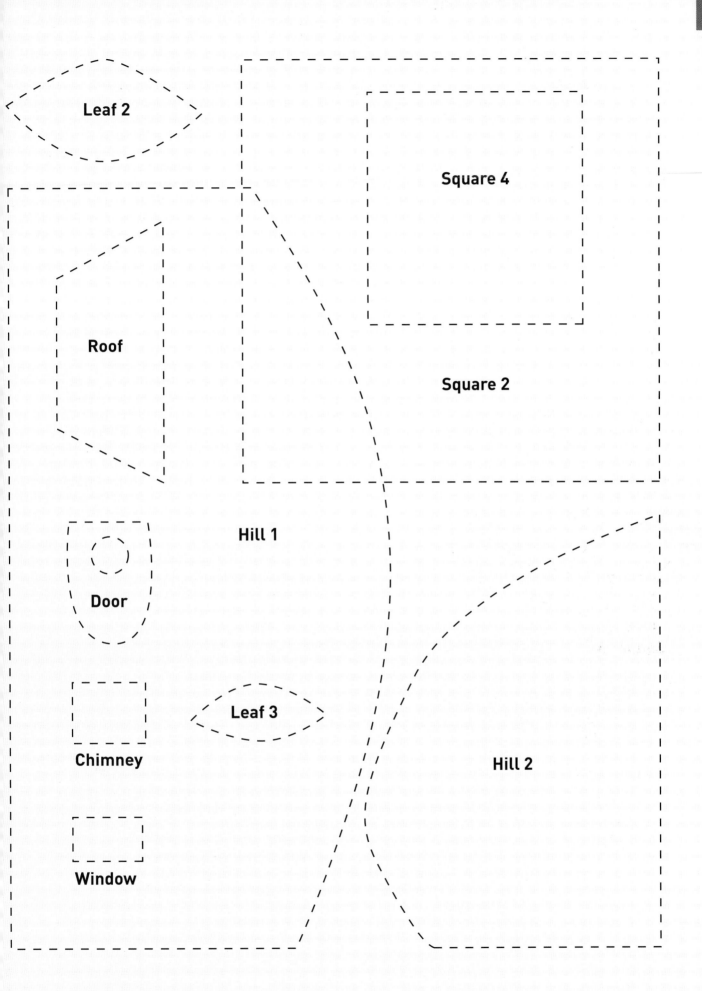

Leaf 2

Square 4

Roof

Square 2

Hill 1

Door

Chimney

Leaf 3

Hill 2

Window

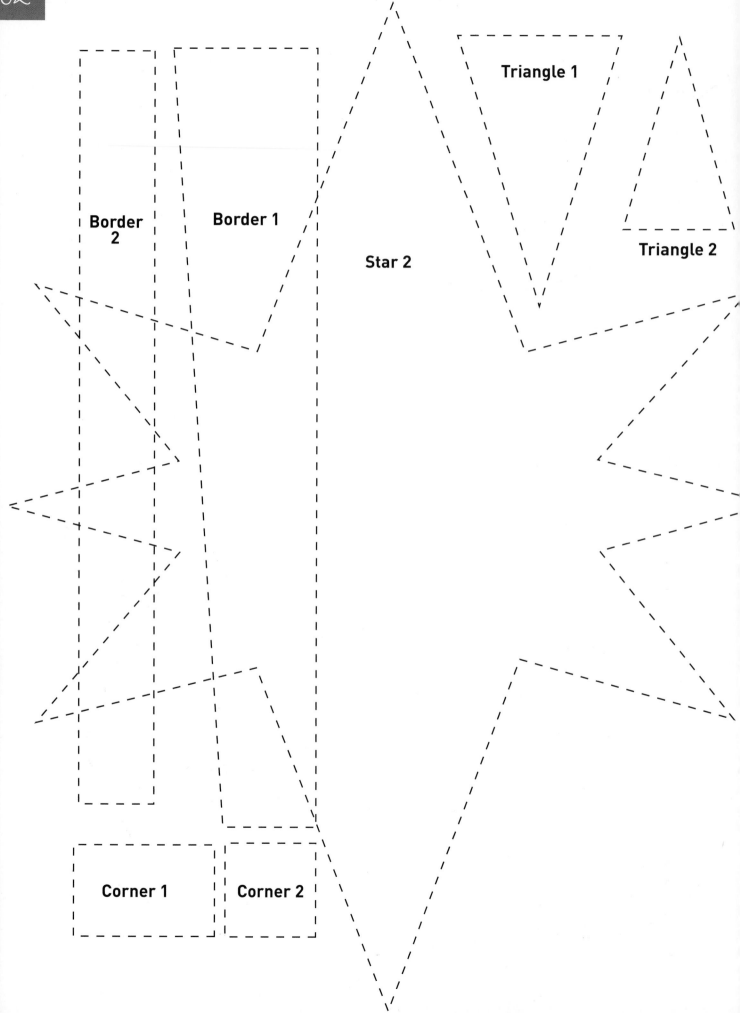

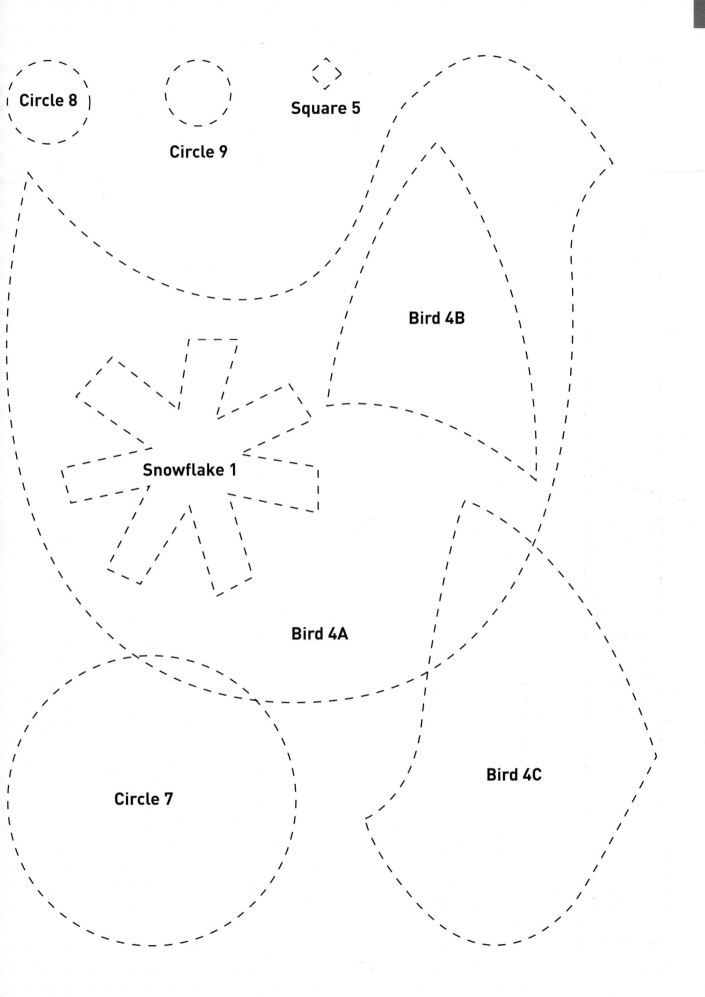

Circle 8

Circle 9

Square 5

Bird 4B

Snowflake 1

Bird 4A

Circle 7

Bird 4C

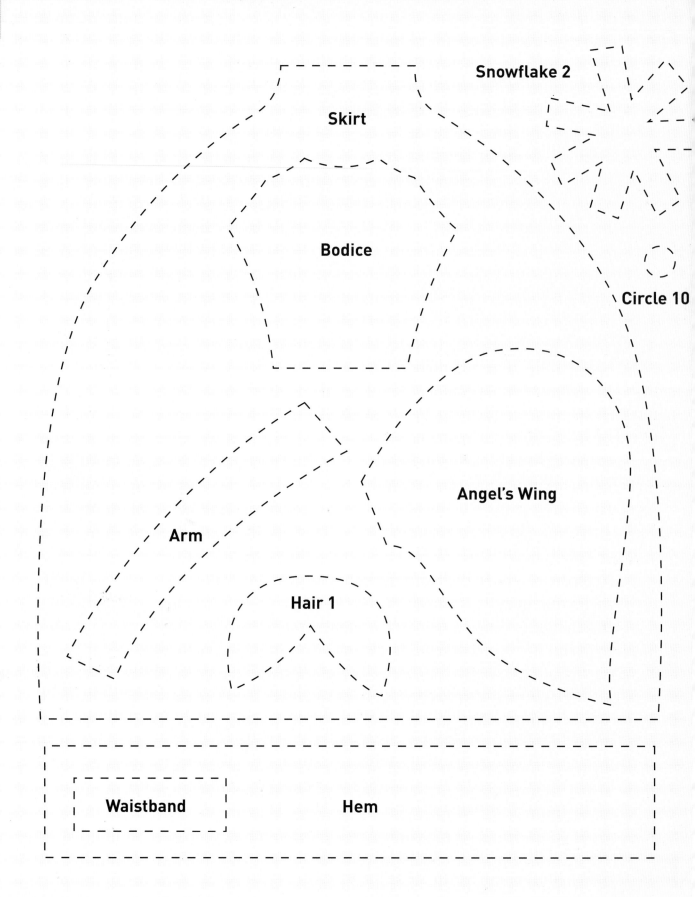

Skirt

Snowflake 2

Bodice

Circle 10

Arm

Angel's Wing

Hair 1

Waistband

Hem

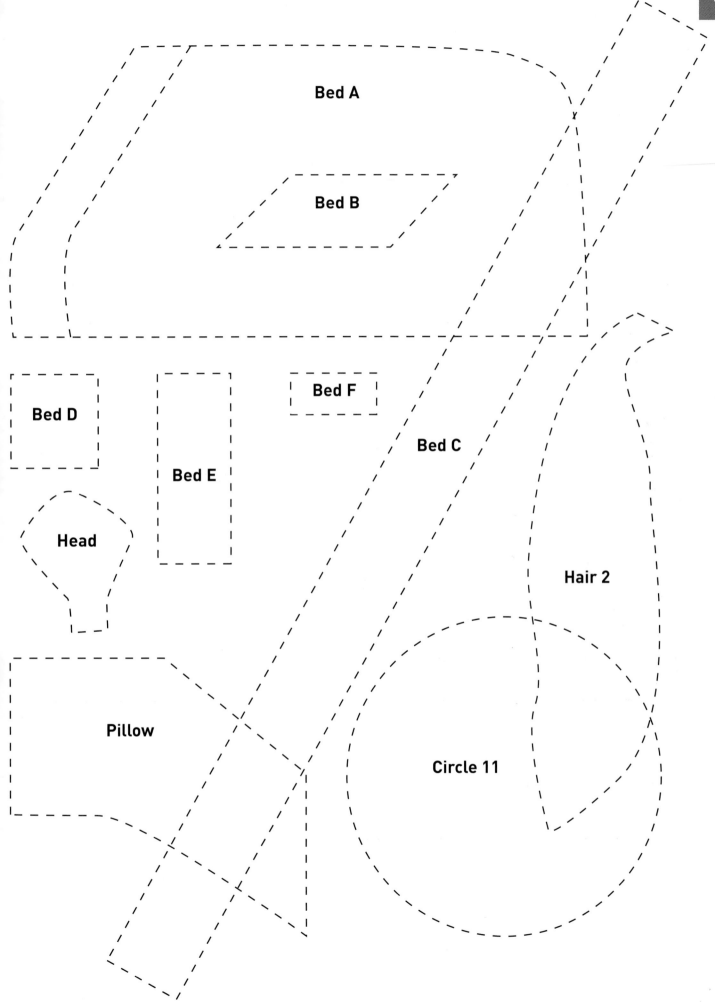

Bed A

Bed B

Bed D

Bed F

Bed C

Bed E

Head

Hair 2

Pillow

Circle 11

Mattress 1

Mattress 2

Mattress 3

Mattress 4

Mattress 5

Mattress 6

Mattress 7

Mattress 8